Chicken

a comic cat memoir

Chicken: A Comic Cat Memoir by Terese Jungle

First edition: January 2016.

All content—including story, writing, drawing, lettering, and photography—is by Terese Jungle. Book/album covers on pages 35 and 51 are re-drawn parodies. Art from other original sources: background image excerpts on page 53 (second and fourth frames) are by artist TomX; background tree painting on page 53 (second frame) by Dan Burns; background image on page 46 by Paul Moran; watermelon painting on page 31 by Bernie Jungle; childhood drawings on pages 35, 61, and 62 by Anastasia Jungle-Wagner; and poem on page 71 by Jeff Hull.

Published by t.jungle Design.

t.jungle™

Books may be purchased in quantity by emailing: info@ChickenTheCat.com and use "BOOK ORDER" in the subject line.

Library of Congress Catalog Number: 2015919880

ISBN: 978-0-9762035-9-9 print/paperback
ISBN: 978-0-9762035-0-6 print/hardback
ISBN: 978-0-9762035-1-3 e book

COMICS & GRAPHIC NOVELS | PETS | FAMILY & RELATIONSHIPS | HUMOR | JUVENILE NONFICTION

For the enchanting Ana,
the lovely Jungles,
the courageous Karolina,
and all timeless beings
who crossed our path.

"[Those] destined to meet will do so,
apparently by chance, at precisely the right time."

- Ralph Waldo Emerson

* Thanks *

...to friends herein who not only met Chicken, but inspired us with laughter, creativity, depth, genius, kindness, love, and compassion, for which we'll always be grateful.

Special thanks to my family for their support, encouragement, and feedback. To friends: Mimi Gonzalez Barillas for her wit, wisdom and early feedback and without whose advice there would be no Chicken; Susie Bright for her early review and suggestions; Karen Porier for marketing consulting; Jeff Hull for his poetry; Karen Santelli for writing, editing, and proofreading precision; Bala Gopal Das for Notes contributions; Amr Shalaby for the loving support in the homestretch; to Ana for her love of this tale, her insistence that I finish it, and her regular editorial and visual suggestions along the way; and to the spirit of Chicken herself for finding us at precisely the right time.

Until she found herself spending lots of
time with a friend's cats:

Slimz & Darling

who clearly had special powers.

Around that time, TJ began dreaming about a cat.
It was as if she was low
to the ground ...

...watching it approach
from a distance...

getting
Closer...

and
CLOSER

And closest of all !

In every dream, it was always the same cat: a black and white "tuxedo tabby" with bright green eyes.

Mimi rushed her to an animal shelter,
where they saw:

Tricky Tabbies

Sleek Siamese

Puffball Persians

mini Kitties

All rather adorable
but none the cat
from her dreams.

About a week later, TJ was at her job at Grace Cathedral.* That day, she happened to be on the roof of Cathedral House, taking photos of the "Rose window" when someone yelled from the courtyard:

hey! Anyone want to adopt a cat?!

* a historic landmark in San Francisco. TJ's office was in Cathedral House, built in 1912.

His job was a "verger" who helps with masses and events.

When the black-and-white cat stood,
they could see it was the smallest,
the skinniest, and quivering all
over in a state of fear and excitement.

I guess someone
had to move and
couldn't take their
cats. They've been
living under the
Cathedral House
probably a few
weeks now...
Looks like
the little
black+white
one was busy
finding food
for them all.

Others who worked there arrived on the scene.

Artist/writer
friend, Nan...

That lady whose name
TJ could never remember...

... and Jake, who'd
been at the Cathedral
for, like, 50 years.

19

SPCA = Society for the Prevention of Cruelty to Animals.

All that was left in the bowl when she returned was...

meyou

Before digital photography, you had to put a roll of film into a camera in order to take pictures. The last picture would often be discolored from exposure to light while being loaded. That's what this image was.

[ACTUAL PHOTO]

...a Smile!
She'd eaten all but 10 kibble, left in this exact arrangement.

and so it was love from the start...

They spent that first day gazing at one another in awe, pausing only when the phone rang.

29

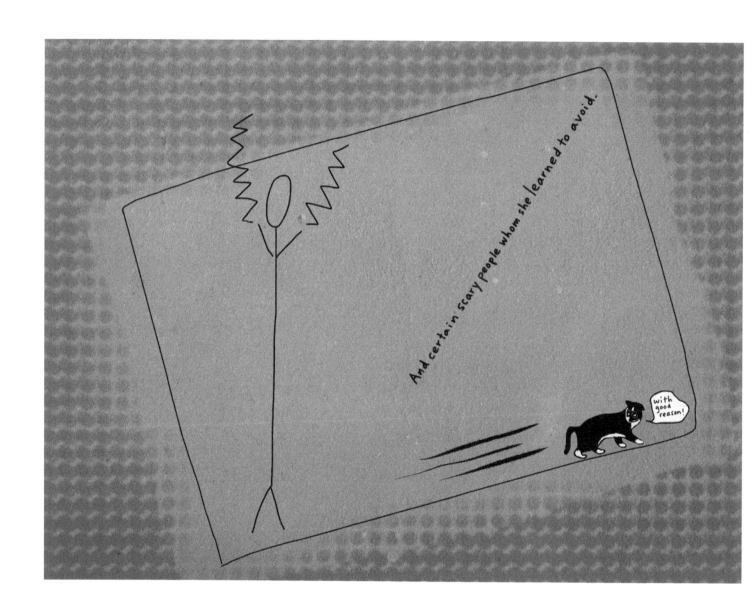

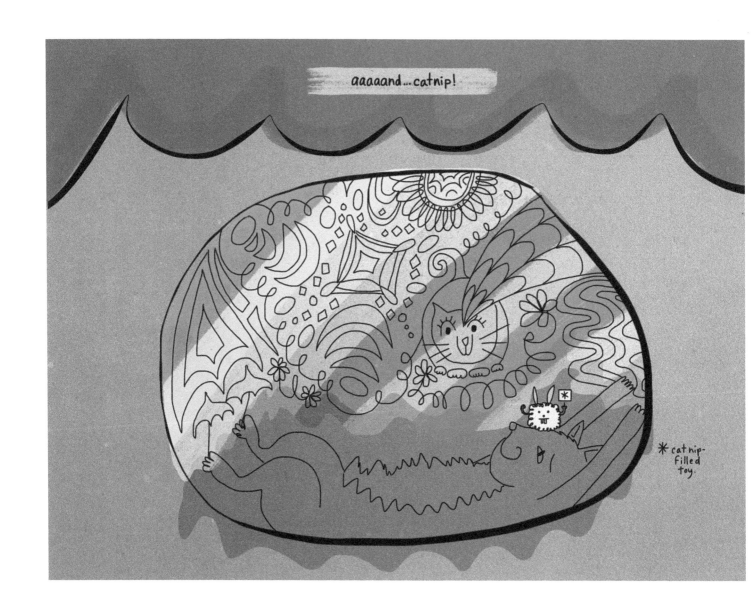

Briefly in the care of "Warners" while TJ drove cross country to settle out West again — this time in Sunny SO. CAL

(a flood of change was upon them)

me → CHICAGO
← old home SAN FRANCISCO
← US soon
LOS ANGELES
NEW MEXICO ← TJ

meanwhile...a stray named "Wayne" arrived

48

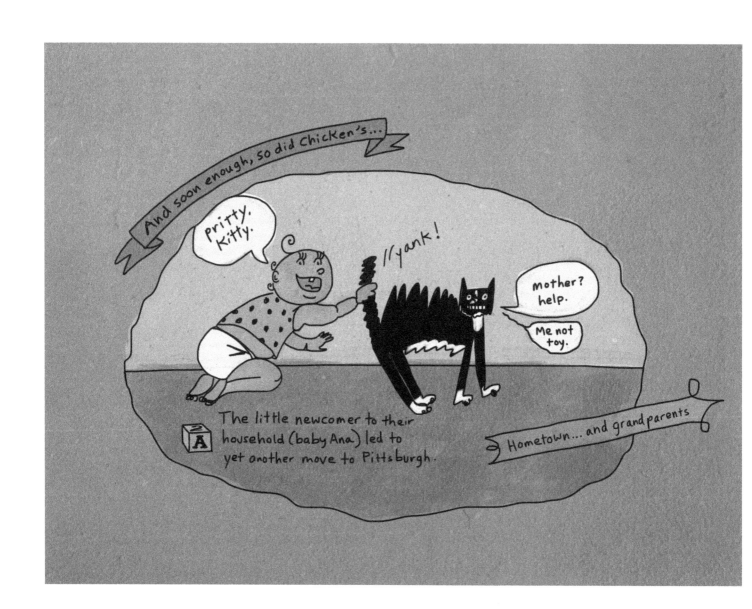

While TJ looked for a new place to live Chicken stayed with TJ's sister, K., whose birds kept Chicken awake all night.

Which then kept K. awake all night.

It only lasted a few months.

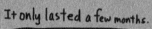

And then one day,

she stayed on the couch from morning until night.

They rushed her to a new vet.

59

Ana looked at puppies, then drew and colored her memories of Chicken.

hopscotch on the porch

salad bowls, salad and glasses of water on the table.

The ol' tail pulling routine.

And then she thought of the unkind—even bullying people who'd made their way into their lives.

Or of the time her litter box was left outside by accident...

And of the times she'd gotten too busy to offer her attention or affection.

And then she felt a surge in her heart, as if a bird flew through her.

That night they found a parting "gift"* from Chicken. While they had never seen a mouse in the house before, there it was, at the foot of the stairs — and not just any old mouse but a pretty one with fancy markings.

aw, thanks, Chicken (I think)

Mipni said that cats kill mice for food when they need to because hunting is their instinct. "Happy cats, who have enough food still do this, but instead of eating it, they "give food" to their humans."

They made a shrine ...

In memory of their sweet friend, surrounding it with protective creatures — some hand-made, some store-bought, and some that came in boxes of tea.

One of Jeff's poems... that fell out of a folder the day after Chicken died — the words reminding TJ of Chicken's cloudy eye and of what it feels like to love someone who has died.
(© Jeff Hall)

photo at 3 years old.

cat face by Ana "to keep her not lonely."

Capsule of ashes, claw, and whisker.

Her first tag.

Hugs and kisses.

Fortune cookie fortune from two days after she died ("li"-the Chinese word for "Chicken.")

Her favorite toy.

Inscrutable maneuver

my eye behind a cloud

regardless of or after

this broken bearing held

Page 5 - Can a Person Get Over a Cat Allergy?

This is not meant as medical advice, however, some people can overcome a cat allergy just by being exposed to cats (or this would not be a true story). It's best to ask an allergist if you have or are seeking ways to improve allergy symptoms. Some people need allergy medication while others must simply avoid cats...only admiring them from a distance. :-}

Page 7 - The Circles Symbol

The three interlocking circles in this scene were meant to simply express the excitement of the cat, of TJ, and of the mysterious force that brought them together. Mimi pointed out that it's a "symbol for God." It was created by St. Patrick after the form of a shamrock to symbolize the Trinity—a central idea to multiple religions.

Page 9 - The "Lovely Lady"

TJ had the distinct pleasure of growing up with a grandma who not only made fun quilts but who was also her first model of a woman entrepreneur. Grandma W. independently owned a small general store, selling basics like milk and bread but also serving as a post office and—best of all for us grand kids—a penny candy store! Oh, and she also had a chihuahua named Cookie.

Page 10 - Was Mimi's Hair Really That Big?

No. But close. Mainly it was an easy way to express her large personality and humor.

Page 13 - The Roof? Really?

Uh...yep. TJ's job was design of all print materials for the Cathedral—things like newsletters and books. They didn't have a good photo of the "rose window" (the name, in architecture, for that kind of circular, segmented window) so TJ headed to the roof to take one.

Page 23 - The SPCA/ASPCA

Pittsburgh shelters like The Western PA Humane Society or Animal Friends are great places to adopt pets. The American Society for the Prevention of Cruelty to Animals also has shelters. Founded in New York in 1866, the ASPCA works tirelessly to help pets find homes so sometimes this is the best place to help your pet find you!

Page 30 - The Chicken Sound

On further investigation into the "bak" sound that earned Chicken her name, TJ only found it called a "chirping" said to emulate bird sounds for hunting prey. But on searching cat videos, she could find none that clucked quite like Chicken's authentic chicken sound.

Page 38 — Chicken's Dream

A parody of *The Place Where Earth and Heaven Meet*, from astrologer Flammarion's 1888 *Popular Meteorology*. The original image's human figure was replaced with a cat and its central tree was replaced with a stalk of catnip.

Page 40 — More About Catnip

Catnip is a plant named as such because cats seem to love it. In fact, contact with it can make them act a bit crazy, causing such unusual behavior as excessive purring, rolling on the catnip itself, wild leaping about or just lazily "spacing out."

Page 41 — What's that Art?

Just some early experiments by TJ, inspired by art of the surrealist movement.

Page 43 — HackeySnax?

This was a joke company made up by TJ and her co-workers at the time...an absurd idea for a toy like the famous one of a similar name, only in edible food shapes for post-play snacking.

Page 43 — The Random Angel

During this period, TJ and friend Nan collaborated on "Gracie," an angel doll and story that was the product of another TJ dream.

Page 43 — The Other Angel

A part of a TJ collage made shortly before moving from San Francisco to Chicago in pursuit of a higher degree.

Page 44 — A Kinetic Sculptor

...is one who makes sculptures that move. In this case, they were metal bowls and other parts that were not only interesting to look at but were mechanized to make cool sounds.

Page 46 — Cats and Grapes?

Cats aren't supposed to like sweets, and some sources such as a vet we asked, even say that grapes and raisins are toxic to both cats and dogs and can lead to kidney failure(!) While Chicken never showed an interest in grapes, Ubi loved them and was allowed to eat them because his owner hadn't heard of any danger in it. Then again, Ubi also liked potato chips and drinking his water from a running tap instead of a bowl, so there's that. :-)

Page 47 — Picasso? Well, No.

If this image looks familiar it's because it parodies Pablo Picasso's famous self-portrait as well as the hand in another of his paintings, *Le Reve* (*The Dream*). This artist friend's energy and enthusiasm just begged for some Picasso-ing up.

Page 48 — Background Words

This writing was intended to add to both texture and mood... to express a friend absorbed in his own thoughts in a creative but chaotic time. Was Chicken helping Warners while TJ was on the road or the other way around? Either way, Chicken would soon re-join her nomadic mama by way of air cargo travel.

Page 48 — That Orange Cat

Wayne's expression is modeled after Orphan Annie because he was an orphan who wandered onto TJ's porch (and in very bad shape). She named him "Wayne" and Warners took him home. His upstairs neighbor took such a liking to the orange cat, that when she moved, she took Wayne with her! Warners was ok with it, though, considering himself a foster parent to the much better match of the cat with his cat-napping neighbor. So this was a case where a cat had to find its person through two other people first!

Page 53 — The Blue Face

The two pictured in front of this face are Bala Gopol Das and Lalita Sundari who are students of "Vaishnavism," the consciousness movement that worships Krishna as God, said to be "the personification of absolute truth and the source of all reality." He is blue because it's the color we associate with things that are beyond our perception, such as the sky or the ocean. Because people from all walks of life are attracted to blue, it's also a color of all-inclusiveness.

Page 55 — Those T-shirts

Yes, more silliness. These are inside jokes among TJ's family. One is of her aunt who orders at the deli by saying "half pound/half pound" (eg: "Cheddar, provolone: half pound/half pound") and while there's no real reason to be amused by this, TJ was. In another, TJ's cousin Dan who shares her love of joke punch lines (yes, free of their jokes) wears a message of support. Then there is little big kid, cousin Jonah, in his *Frizzball from Outer Space* shirt (frizzball.com) and on the end is TJ's good friend Karen who left her heart in New Orleans (a.k.a. NOLA).

Page 57 — Grandma V.

This is the "courageous Karolina" mentioned in the dedication, or TJ's Grandma V. She immigrated from Slovakia when she was 18. Usually preferring to dress up for photos, she disliked this shot of herself. It was TJ's favorite because she felt it perfectly captured her fiery spirit, warm affection, and playful humor. Although she has "gone on to other adventures," TJ still feels her presence vividly every day.

Page 69 — What "Died" Means

There are many different be-
liefs about what happens (and
what we choose to tell our
children about what happens)
when we die. Thank you respect-
fully for appreciating that the
author's belief may differ from
yours or that of your religion.

Page 71 — Animals in Tea Boxes?

Kind of like prizes in cereal
boxes (but way higher quali-
ty), Rose Tea has a tradition
of giving away "Wade Whimsies,"
animal figurines made by En-
gland's George Wade Pottery
Company, in specially marked
boxes of tea. Sometimes this
called for buying a whole extra
box of tea just to get an extra
figurine!

Page 72 — Those Trees

This is a photo montage
created by the author in 2008,
entitled *1111*. The original
photo was taken in Highland
Park on the East End of Pittsburgh, which so happens to
be where TJ's next cat found
her and Ana. It was digitally
manipulated to create a kalei-
doscopic effect that reminded
the author of double elevens—a
numerological sequence said to
symbolize self-knowledge, pos-
itivity, and new beginnings,
making it the perfect image
for the end of this story.

This image and other
illustrations from the
book are available as
prints on the website,
as is *The Frizzball
From Outer Space* toy
(for both cats and
their humans :-)

www.ChickenTheCat.com

CPSIA information can be obtained
at www.ICGtesting.com
Printed in the USA
BVHW010140150423
662426BV00015B/197